# STOP the Compromise in Ten Easy Steps

**Also by Georgiana Preskar:**

*White Privilege and The Wheel of Oppression: The Hoax of the Century*

*Diversity Addiction: The Cause and The Cure*

*Seeds of Deception: Planting Destruction of America's Children*

# STOP the Compromise in Ten Easy Steps
## *A Return to Authentic Rule of Law*

Georgiana Preskar

iUniverse, Inc.
Bloomington

# STOP the Compromise in Ten Easy Steps
## A Return to Authentic Rule of Law

*Copyright © 2011 by Georgiana Preskar*

*All rights reserved. No part of this book may be used or reproduced by any means, graphic, electronic, or mechanical, including photocopying, recording, taping or by any information storage retrieval system without the written permission of the publisher except in the case of brief quotations embodied in critical articles and reviews.*

*iUniverse books may be ordered through booksellers or by contacting:*

*iUniverse*
*1663 Liberty Drive*
*Bloomington, IN 47403*

www.iuniverse.com
*1-800-Authors (1-800-288-4677)*

*Because of the dynamic nature of the Internet, any web addresses or links contained in this book may have changed since publication and may no longer be valid. The views expressed in this work are solely those of the author and do not necessarily reflect the views of the publisher, and the publisher hereby disclaims any responsibility for them.*

*Any people depicted in stock imagery provided by Thinkstock are models, and such images are being used for illustrative purposes only.*

*Certain stock imagery © Thinkstock.*

ISBN: 978-1-4620-2633-3 (sc)
ISBN: 978-1-4620-2634-0 (ebk)

*Printed in the United States of America*

*iUniverse rev. date: 07/27/2011*

"We must reject the idea that every time a law's broken, society is guilty rather than the lawbreaker. It is time to restore the American precept that each individual is accountable for his actions."

**Ronald Reagan**

"Laws are made for men of ordinary understanding and should, therefore, be construed by the ordinary rules of common sense. Their meaning is not to be sought for in metaphysical subtleties, which may make anything mean everything or nothing at pleasure."

**Thomas Jefferson**

"The belief in a God All Powerful wise and good, is so essential to the moral order of the world and to the happiness of man, that arguments which enforce it cannot be drawn from too many sources nor adapted with too much solicitude to the different characters and capacities impressed with it."

**James Madison**

# DEDICATION

To my husband of 36 years for being the cowboy in my life.

In memory of James Arness (1923-2011) whose outstanding portrayal of the mythical Marshal Dillon in *Gunsmoke* continues to provide examples of authentic rule of law.

# FORWARD

The galloping of Silver's hoofs still lingers in my mind. As a child, our living room radio was a focal point of family gatherings. Listening to *The Lone Ranger* ignited our vivid imaginations to places unknown by most of today's children. Playtime became my reality and each day I grabbed my pretend horse Silver, as well as my cowgirl hat, boots, toy gun, and holster and rode the backyard plains fighting for the good guys. It was a time when children learned right from wrong based on strong teachings through family, schools, church, and the media. Diversity was a natural part of life. No one had to enforce it or insist on compromise.

In 2002 I heard the pounding hoofs again when I discovered Seeking Educational Equity and Diversity (SEED), the worldwide authority on transformation education. After researching SEED and other enforced diversity programs, I knew that our country was in danger. I had to ride the range again, but this time delivering truth through my books, speaking engagements, and grassroots' organizations. People had to know that well-managed deception and tools of change caused diversity addiction that was stealing our liberties and freedom of conscience. My imaginary horse and cowgirl attire became my inner spirit as the attempt to reach others became a reality.

Enforced diversity teaches that all ideas, values, morals, ethics, lifestyles, religions, and personally held beliefs hold equal value, but people who doubt it, are not treated equally. In fact they are labeled bigots, hateful, and homophobes and not protected under anti-bullying laws unless they accept redefined diversity. Let's reverse the equation, for common sense tells us that all people are created equal, but that ideas, values, morals, ethics, lifestyles, religions, and personally held beliefs are not equal. For diversity to be true to its purpose it must accept Judeo-Christians, European descendants, and traditional patriots (The Big Three) complete with their beliefs.

Daily life has become strenuous for The Big Three because their First Amendment and civil rights are taken away from them on a daily basis. Those who buy into redefined diversity are fooled into believing they have gained their rights. White Privilege and Wheel of Oppression education thrives on the mass production of victims who demand entitlements. Eager learners of all ages crave acceptance and love and are easily swayed into getting them through emotions that push them to compromise their beliefs. We now have anti-American voters as young as 18 who encourage "feel good" laws that are not in line with God's authority, natural law, the Constitution, and plain old common sense.

America is in grave danger of losing its identity. What will we tell our children and grandchildren one day when they ask why we did nothing to save America? Many people don't know what to do. Their direction is curtailed by busy days and demands that make it difficult to find answers and easier ways to make a difference that will fit into their lifestyles. Some people do not want to get into debates with others because of fear, rejection, and uncertainty of how to present the facts. Most want to take charge of their lives again and say "No" to government. It is an easy process to STOP the compromise.

At last, a simple guide for everyone that is concerned about the future of America. The Ten-Step STOP program is also uplifting. It's time for everyone to enjoy the process of taking back our nation. Learn about authentic rule of law and how to respond daily to those who try to engage you in feel-good rhetoric to rob you of your beliefs. Protect everyone's liberty and don't compromise.

Know how to decipher what stages of brainwashing have molded a person's beliefs. Make your communication easier. Know how to control your emotions to give you the advantage. You will learn how to stand in truth by a quick response that will leave your opponent with something to think about. The satisfaction that you have given a simple fact that you declare as truth and not debatable provides a natural high. All that is needed is for you to make the decision to read on and take action.

Whatever your reasons, your background, or your level of knowledge, this book will give you what you need to defend this great nation through the STOP Movement. Ride the range again in truth and STOP the Compromise!

# ACKNOWLEDGMENTS

Foremost is my ongoing gratefulness to God who gave us a perfect plan to live by with the result of the authentic rule of law.

I am thankful to our children Michael and Michelle for the joy of raising them and cherished memories of family traditions.

Thank you to our four grandchildren Angela, Michael, Monica, and Michael who bring awareness of God's most precious gift, life.

My gratitude to my Dad who at 92 years old offers me wisdom and hope and continues to be an example of how old age still holds purpose in life.

Thank you to the military for dedication and courage in standing for the true American way in the face of a changing nation.

I am grateful to my family, friends, and colleagues that work to STOP the compromise of truth.

Thank you to Teri for years dedicated to protect the children for survival of America.

I thank our daughter-in-law Josilyn for the many hours of editing and her support of my undertaking.

# Table of Contents

DEDICATION ........................................................................... vii

FORWARD ................................................................................ ix

ACKNOWLEDGMENTS ........................................................ xi

STEP 1:   KNOW YOUR OPPONENT ............................... 1

STEP 2:   THE STOP MOVEMENT ................................... 4

STEP 3:   GOD'S AUTHORITY ......................................... 6

STEP 4:   NATURAL LAW ............................................... 10

STEP 5:   THE CONSTITUTION ..................................... 15

STEP 6:   COMMON SENSE ........................................... 21

STEP 7:   RELIGIOUS AND SOCIAL RESPONSES ...... 24

STEP 8:   POLITICAL RESPONSES ................................ 39

STEP 9:   ECONOMIC RESPONSES .............................. 52

STEP 10:  STOP THE COMPROMISE ............................ 60

ABOUT THE AUTHOR ......................................................... 63

REFERENCES ........................................................................ 65

# STEP 1
# KNOW YOUR OPPONENT

Welcome to the first step of the STOP Movement. Knowing the opponent is critical to bringing a halt to compromise in your life. Some people have a tough time with decisions; don't be one of them. Take charge of your life and become secure in your actions and thoughts based on fact. When a person or group opposes the truth then it is a fair assumption that they are your opponent. This revelation becomes apparent at some point during various interactions. It can be early on in a conversation or hidden for a length of time. Keep your mind alert and you will know your opponent by three things: listening, observation, and emotions.

Before a person can engage in a competition of any sort, they must know their opponent. This is just common sense. The winner obviously is the one with the best plan. The intent of this book is not to educate as to the factors that have or continue to cause destruction of America for they are covered in my previous books. This book deals with the here and now and the recovery from entitlement nonsense that allows others to steal liberties by our compromise.

A simple definition of compromise is a resolution of differences in which each side makes concessions. In order to compromise there must be a foundation of common interests. One cannot negotiate if both sides are too much in contrast with each other. Truth cannot be compromised. When people give-in to any part of their position, they come out of absolutes and open themselves to emotional appeal. The other person can easily push them into a defensive mode rather than an offensive one. Your position in truth is then diminished.

Take note that a great part of our day is spent interacting with others. So wherever you go is an opportune moment to converse with people. This is your opportunity to pick up on clues as to whether the person is an opponent. First you must become a careful listener. If you hear particular words and phrases, you'll get a fair idea about the person's worldview. Compromised people will draw attention to their attitudes by repetitions of particular words. They will state certain beliefs about them which will indicate their non-traditional worldview.

The words and phrases include the following: tolerance, diversity, empowering, embrace, feel, the loving thing to do, politically correct, hateful, consensus, compromise for common good, crossing bridges, coming together, agree to disagree, globalism, green movement, global warming, mother earth, father sky, a woman's right to choose, abortion, euthanasia, over-population, women's rights, gay, lesbian, gender 1, gender 2, partners, homophobe, same-sex marriage, sex-Ed, animal rights, earth rights, sustainable development, redistribution, entitlement, community organizers, oppression, social justice, white privilege, and all things hold equal value.

Second, you must be observant of others' physical appearance as mentioned earlier. A person dresses a certain way for a reason; many times it does describe them as a person. For example, why is a woman wearing seductive clothing? If she is married and a Christian showing cleavage then what illogical reasoning is she using? If a person has multiple piercings and tattoos you know they are not concerned with tradition, and may enjoy a more whimsical attitude toward life.

Third, involves emotions. When feel-good rhetoric rules over reason it is clear the person is using improper reasoning. It is very important to listen to people not just for words, but also for clues as to how this person is embedded in the subject matter personally. It makes a difference if there is a personal interest in the subject matter, such as a woman who had an abortion, for then the topic will take on a definite emotional feel. Listening will also give clues as to the influencing factors that led this person to their beliefs.

The above steps of observation are useful in everyday situations to keep you and your loved ones safe from change agents. Many are trained in deception and have successfully compromised persons and groups. We can be one step ahead of them by recognizing it. An important agent of change is brainwashing. It needs attention. There are four stages of brainwashing. It exists in diversity and sensitivity programs across the country.

The stages of brainwashing make compromise easy, for it can happen subtly while even watching TV. The media is great at persuasion, for that is what sales are all about. Once you are familiar with the strategy of brainwashing you will understand how far along your opponent is on the road to being a change agent, which is working toward your compromise. You must keep his goal in mind while you are conversing. Below are the four stages of brainwashing:

**Aspiration:** This is a strong desire to improve oneself, the community, and or the world. People are moved to make the world a better place to live in. By giving up some of their beliefs to make things right for others, they become more loving people. Many times a wrong becomes right with this illogical reasoning.

**Meditation:** The purpose is to calm the mental state. A person must get rid of preconceived thoughts and ideas. This can occur by watching TV, playing music, daydreaming, programmed meditations, or indoctrination methodology. People can be swayed while in these situations.

**Disorientation:** A paradox can be set up to make a person question their beliefs. Presenting controversial information to youngsters is dangerous because they do not have mature awareness to handle it. College students, as well as adults, can also be swayed by paradoxes, making something absurd actually real.

**Re-orientation:** This takes place through peer pressure and false friendship. Once the paradox is accepted, peer pressure is a strong motivator to change behavior. With a sense of community, loving-kindness and acceptance, people's desire to change becomes strong. The compromise becomes easy at this junction.

Become familiar with the stages. They are used frequently and are vital to the success of Marxist change. See how many of them you can identify on a daily basis. Observe groups carefully in order to understand their position. It is challenging to observe another person so you can respond confidently in truth. Everyone compromises on irrelevant issues, but when compromise affects God's law there is automatic chaos. Proper reasoning and facts must be introduced. This can be accomplished through the STOP Movement.

# STEP 2
# THE STOP MOVEMENT

STOP signs and signals have a purpose, to bring to a halt. Automobile, bicycle, and pedestrian accidents are frequently caused by people not paying attention to the signals. Whatever the reason it can be fatal for a person and for others involved in it, or affected by it. Accidents can change the course of a person, family, or group's life and it will never be the same for those involved in such a scenario.

STOP is a powerful tool to keep people safe; yet people avoid it in many areas of their life. Compromise aids them in the process. They move out of absolutes and slide right through the STOP sign. Many refuse to heed its warnings, but for those who recognize the dangers affecting America, they are the ones that must bring awareness to the forefront. We must push the STOP sign in front of not only ourselves, but others. When we take control of the situation it produces an adrenaline rush that everyone is familiar with and enjoys.

This is the rush I experienced while interacting at a recent wedding. The man read my first book and engaged me in conversation regarding adoption of children by homosexuals. All clues indicated he wanted me to compromise. I however did not bend. Adopting my STOP attitude, I listened carefully, withdrew from emotions, answered with a quick response, and stopped. My opponent had nothing to say. The timing was perfect. The music was beginning and my husband rescued me from debate by a dance.

The purpose of the STOP Movement is straightforward, to STOP compromising the truth. Everyone is capable of a STOP attitude on a daily basis. How you ask? Let me tell you what changed my life forever, a four day self-defense gun class at Front Sight Firearms Training Institute. The daily 10 hour class was grueling, requiring focus on facts and attention to safety. The first night upon return to the hotel room I wanted to escape home. Though I am a high energy person, I was exhausted.

Discipline found me the next morning. I was excited about the new day and what I would learn. It became fun after a while and we were even able to shoot pop up figures dependent on instant decisions as to whether they were the good guy or the bad guy. The third day we had a class that inspired me to make some good concrete changes in my life. We learned about the legality of shooting someone when they enter your home; could a person actually do it and when would they shoot.

A remarkable class for one very important thing we learned was to let the intruder know we meant business. We had to push our arm out in front of us and at the same time shouting STOP to them. The instructor asked a girl to stand up and demonstrate. She meekly did so, but certainly not enough to stop any one. She had to repeat it again and again. Eventually she was able to scream it out and forcefully push her arm forward so that the person knew she meant business.

An individual must decide before such an incident occurs if they will take the life of an intruder. If so, then quick action is required if he does not stop. One cannot doubt their decision. In fact many people, including police officers, die because they give the bad guy a second chance. America must not die. People aware of destructive forces must be bold in their actions to save this great nation. They must not hesitate. The STOP Movement is vital for recovery.

People compromise because they do not know how to say "STOP." My new quest began as did my husbands. We found that by using this technique in our relationship we were able to avoid arguments before they began by a simple STOP. Everyone can use these tactics. When dealing with an opponent, one must be clear in a strong STOP attitude. If you love America, then you know the importance of saving it from destruction. Future generations are dependent on us.

Listen, observe, and limit time with an opponent. Do not get involved with emotional debate. Liberals rely on them for your compromise. Deliver your quick response with confidence and STOP the falsehood. Let the truth be known. When you stay in your absolutes there is a powerful message delivered. You can be part of an important movement which will impact others on a daily basis. Read on for the foundation of the STOP Movement.

# STEP 3
# GOD'S AUTHORITY

God's authority is supreme and absolute. It's our job to elevate His authentic rule of law to number one in priority. All other laws need to be clarified as to their authenticity. Sounds strange at first, for how can a law not be law? If the law does not coexist in harmony with God's Law, natural law, and Constitutional Law then it is not authentic law and we have chaos. To let go and let God be the final authority is uplifting. It brings liberty and freedom to all. We must discern the validity of laws.

In order for a society to harmoniously function it must have laws to live by. Some people say that we can live a good moral life without religion. They are the same ones who have overwhelmed our system with unnecessary man made laws, or the Humanist Manifestos. For a society to function smoothly they must distinguish right from wrong and need a reference point. If humans decide what is right then laws can be changed by humans that also seek whatever feels right.

An authority reference point must be determined that is not human. This must come from an all perfect being. There is proof of a God if one chooses to believe it by simply using a thought process of proper reasoning. "I exist; I am special, so how could I come from nothing?" Mankind must have come from someone that is extraordinary and powerful.

The average person knows an inanimate object does not create them. Only a Creator who knows and understands cognitive processes could produce the same kind of being. There is also proof of a God when we observe there are no intermediary links from ape to mankind. Reasoning tells humanity that the order of the universe is proof of a higher being; the complexity of human DNA is the best support for belief in God. Atheists refuse to use this reasoning and choose to deny God.

God makes sense. A perfect Creator is an example of total goodness and the reference point needed to determine evil. He gives simple principles to live by. Through the use of educated men, scholars, facts of history, and the Bible, America based its beginnings on that which offered all men the freedom of will and conscience through the Judeo-Christian God. This is tradition and fact and nothing can change the truth. Whether a believer or not, the facts speak for themselves.

From the founding of this great nation, the belief in God and Jesus was at the forefront of the establishment of America. Historians find that our Founding Fathers used and cited more references from the Bible than from other sources. The Christian basis of our documents sets America aside from all other nations and countries. We serve as a beacon of freedom for all.

"We the People," in the Constitution preamble, will forever be a reminder that America is able to stand alone because of a higher authority on which our rules are based. They cannot change. Those seeking to transform America are increasingly using tyrannical methods to attack citizens and the unchanging principles upon which America was founded. The Ten Commandments are attacked frequently, but they cannot be erased from the rule of law.

The ACLU has tried for years to eliminate monuments and inspirational locations that display the Ten Commandments. Out of sight, out of mind is their goal. They have disrespected God, our military, churches, and America's tradition. It does not work, for the truth cannot be dismissed. The Ten Commandments are a part of this nation as long as it exists.

Remember nothing can change the truth. The Scriptures were inspired by God and are also important in the development of the authentic rule of law. The biblical principle of Sovereign authority of God, not state or man, is the basis for the Mayflower Compact, Declaration of Independence, Constitution, currency, oaths, the mention of God in 50 state constitutions, and the Pledge of Allegiance. Some of the Biblical references are below:

> Exodus 20:3... The First Commandment, "You shall have no other Gods before me."

Exodus 18:16…"Whenever they have a dispute, it is brought to me, and I decide between the parties and inform them of God's decrees and laws."

Psalm 83:18…"Let them know that you, whose name is the Lord-that you alone are the Most High over all the earth."

Deuteronomy 10:20…"Fear the Lord your God and serve Him."

Daniel 4:32…"Seven times will pass by for you until you acknowledge that the Most High is sovereign kingdoms of me."

Acts 5:29…"Peter and the other apostles replied: 'We must obey God rather than man."

Timothy 6:15…"…which God will bring about in His own time, God, the blessed and only Ruler, the King of kings and Lord of lords…"

Deuteronomy 8:19-20…"If you ever forget the Lord your God and follow other gods and worship and bow down to them, I testify against you today that be destroyed. Like the nations the Lord destroyed before you, so you will be destroyed for not obeying the Lord your God."

John 1:17… "…For the law was given through Moses; grace and truth came through Jesus Christ…"

The facts clearly show that the Founding Fathers were not advocating people to follow a particular religion or even lifestyle. Unalienable rights given by God protect people from a tyrannical government that could easily take away our individual freedom. Laws from God and natural law give us freedom, not take it away. We must never apologize to anyone for our beliefs for they are the truth. We must be excited about this and use it for the benefit of our opponent.

Remember to remove yourself from the final authority on controversial topics. Leave the supremacy to God. He is all-powerful and has the final say about the issues of debate. Instead of getting upset at social functions, let God be the authority. You can deliver the message with conviction. Do not be afraid to use His name; give credit where due. It is best to answer with the truth of God's authority as the most powerful in decision making.

Let me give you an example to think about. Once, while attending a 70th birthday party, I met a woman for the first time that was in her 60's. In the course of interaction she mentioned that she was a Christian. As the conversation progressed she stated her daughter had moved in with a man. I asked her how she handled this as a Christian. It truly sparked something in her. She began to raise her voice stating that she herself got married without having premarital sex. She made it clear she was unhappy, got divorced, and wanted better for her daughter. Her words revealed an opportune moment.

God's authority had to be mentioned. I simply thanked her for sharing her thoughts and then asked. "Do you believe God is all truthful and cannot tell a lie?" "Of course," she said. My response was, "He must mean it when He says that we are supposed to follow His rules. I for one would not want to stand before Him on judgment day and say I thought I knew better than Him on such subject matter."

She had absolutely nothing to say, but just looked at me a bit bewildered. The topic stopped and the buffet line was beginning. It was the perfect opportunity for me and I used it to leave the scene. Her blank stare led me to believe she was thinking. I will never know the direction this moved her, but I do know that it was an opportune moment. I had to judge the time, know she would hear my words, and act quickly to make a statement that ended in His authority.

Whether the person you are conversing with is a believer or not, we must make it clear that America uses God as its reference point. A statement of truth was made. The rest of the party was a good one. One sometimes wonders if it could have been said differently, but not this time.

# STEP 4
# NATURAL LAW

Natural law is derived from nature and based on a higher power. It's a simple premise of knowing what's right naturally by simply looking around and figuring it out through proper reasoning. It serves as a common sense way to live and a base for civil law. Long ago, learned men realized that there was an all-powerful source that put things together in a way that could not come about just by chance. For those who choose to ignore it or are arrogant enough to believe there is no natural law, they must suffer the consequences of their decisions. We must say STOP to those who make a mockery of it, by passing laws out of line with it.

In the past, natural law held an important place in law schools in America. Rules of conduct inherent in human nature are essential and binding on human society. Now there is little discussion of it. It's up to dedicated citizens to reeducate this nation in the truth of natural law. God gifted man with the tools to research, assimilate, and use wisdom in leading others to the truth. The Founding Fathers chose wisely the writings most beneficial for forming a Constitution that would secure liberty and happiness. One of them was Marcus Tullius Cicero (106…43 B.C.), a learned man, leading lawyer, and philosopher, as well as holding the highest position of state, Roman Consul.

His writings had a profound effect on the outcome of the Declaration and the Constitution. He was not a Jew or a Christian, but his famous books *The Republic* and *The Law* indicate that he knew that if a nation were to base itself upon natural law, it would be the best ever. Natural law is common sense reasoning by human beings that is in line with the Creator and makes sense. He has endowed us with this ability because He told us that He made us in His image and likeness. Thus as human beings we have a responsibility to use this power in a correct way since it is the true law. Cicero states the following about this law:

> True law is right reason in agreement with nature; it is of universal application, unchanging and everlasting; it summons to duty by its commands, and averts from wrongdoing by its prohibitions. It is a sin to try to alter this law, nor is it allowable to repeal any part of it, and it is impossible to abolish it entirely. We cannot be freed from its obligations by senate or people and we need not ourselves for an expounder or interpreter of it...

One could write volumes on the natural law. The intent of this chapter is to make readers keenly aware of it. Your rights come from God's authority and natural law, not from legislation and man-made laws. The right exists first and law is put in place to protect the rights. This is a very important fact. Natural law as a term of legal art was based on Catholic thought in the twelfth Century. Gratian's *Treatise of the Discordant Canons*, a source of various canon laws, states the following:

> Natural law is common to all nations because it exists everywhere through natural instinct, not because of any enactment. It includes the union of men and women, the succession and rising of children, the identical liberty of all in the acquisition of those things, which I omit, which are taken from the earth or sea, the return of a thing deposited or of money entrusted, and the repelling of violence by force. This, and anything similar, is never regarded as unjust, but is held to be natural and equitable.

The Founding Fathers supported this philosophy and were familiar with the famous writers of International law. These writers who contributed to the principles of the Declaration and the Constitution are Baron de Montesquieu, Sir William Blackstone, and John Locke. Many people do not understand natural law because they have never been exposed to it through the writings of the above gentlemen. The facts of natural law are conveniently hidden and people are reeducated in principles contrary to natural instinct. Once again mankind knows in their hearts what the truth is by simply looking at nature. God makes it clear in the Bible that we know in our heart what is right and what is wrong.

Many people deny it and ignore natural law for assorted reasons. It is important that people understand those who are trying to change our unalienable rights via new laws are not in proper reasoning when the laws go against our natural rights. These laws are not authentic and do not protect our rights. Proper reasoning people are not compromised and know deceptive laws because these laws cause chaos. Let's go over some of our unalienable natural rights listed in *The 5000 Year Leap* below:

> The right of self-government; the right to bear arms for self-defense; the right to own, develop, and dispose of property; the right to make personal choices; the right of free conscience; the right to choose a profession; the right to choose a mate; the right to beget one's kind; the right to assemble; the right to petition; the right to free speech; the right to a free press; the right to enjoy the fruits of one's own labor; the right to improve one's position through barter and sale; the right to contrive and invent; the right to explore the natural resources of the earth; the right to privacy; the right to provide personal security; the right to provide nature's necessities-air, food, water, clothing, and shelter; the right to a fair trial; the right of free association; and the right to contract.

Many of the laws made today are out of line with natural law, so we must be aware of the above rights. Sometimes we have to follow unauthentic laws, but in reality there are others we can still speak out against by using our Constitutional rights to defend our unalienable rights. English defenders of human rights were aware of these eleven years before the Declaration of Independence was written. Sir William Blackstone stated the following:

And these great natural rights may be reduced to three principal or primary articles: the right of personal security; the right of personal liberty; and the right of private property; because as there is no other known method of compulsion, or of abridging man's natural free will, but by an infringement or diminution of one or other of these important rights, the preservation of these, inviolate, may justly be said to include the preservation of our civil immunities in their largest and most extensive sense.

We must be bold in our daily awareness of how our freedoms are disappearing. It is only through the individual's commitment to daily reeducation of our people that we can save our liberties for the survival of America. Most importantly once again it is essential that we completely and without reservations understand that our liberties came first and then the law was instituted to protect them. Frederick Bastiat, a French classical liberal theorist, political economist, and member of the French assembly in the mid-19th Century made the following statement:

> Life, liberty, and property do not exist because men have made laws. On the contrary it was the fact that life, liberty, and property existed beforehand that caused men to make laws in the first place.

The American people must wake up. We cannot afford to lose our liberties. Much of the chaos we experience is caused by many laws that are against human nature. Natural law tells us there are two ways to judge good and evil, through instinct and through reasoning. There is a gut feeling that comes on immediately to know right and wrong. Those who speak against homosexuality are accused of being homophobic (fear of homosexuality). Those using proper reasoning about illegal immigration being bad are accused of xenophobia (fear of foreigners). These are false allegations.

One purpose of the STOP Movement is to take a stand on such nonsensical thinking. Liberals are experts at redefining words such as phobias. The real definition of a phobia is a persistent, abnormal, and irrational fear of a specific thing or situation that compels one to avoid it, despite the awareness and reassurance that it is not dangerous. People who are falsely accused of phobias cannot be put in this category because the truth is that there are dangers connected to homosexuality and illegal immigration. This is fact. It's not fabricated.

Moral issues that cause confusion cannot be fixed by multiple new laws, but can be fixed very easily through natural law and proper reasoning. When an unborn baby is being ripped apart and murdered via abortion that is a horror that every person knows is against human nature. When people are confronted with homosexual lifestyles, they are not fearful of it, but know it to be inherently against human nature. It's not a good role model of relationships or family life for our children. When increased taxes and the new health care law rob them of their property, they know it's wrong.

No matter how many laws are passed they cannot solve these problems because they go against all that is inherently human. For those who believe laws contrary to natural law they have a number of things going on to block their ability to see right and wrong. Some of them are fear of rejection; a need for love and acceptance; a family member, friend, or self has identified themselves as homosexual; a person living with guilt of an abortion; people who want something for nothing; and human arrogance that uses flawed reasoning to judge evil as good.

Enforced diversity gives approval of individual inability to follow natural law. We do a grave injustice to those bearing various afflictions, for our silence gives okay to them. In coming years our society will reap the results of redefined diversity. People will be unstable and seek psychotherapy. The serious accusations against those who now stand for traditional moral law must be stopped. When a person or group defends actions and passes laws that are not in line with natural law, then it is our responsibility to say STOP. It also makes sense that our Constitution is in crisis.

# STEP 5
# THE CONSTITUTION

America's second President John Adams stated, "The Constitution is...the greatest single effort of national deliberation that the world has ever seen." Yet it's the best kept secret in America. It remains unknown in content to the majority of Americans. How sad, for our Founding Fathers gave time, property, and even life to write this precious document. Signed into effect on September 17, 1787, it is the most important legal document in American law.

Legislative bills such as the Patient Protection and Affordable Care Act (Obama Care) cause chaos because they're out of line with Constitutional law. The Founders intended the rule of law to protect the rights of all citizens and be applied equally to everyone. There are too many laws not in line with the original intent of our Founding Fathers as stated by James Madison in The Federalist Papers, #62:

> It will be of little avail to the people that the laws are made by men of their own choice, if the laws be so voluminous that they cannot be read, or so incoherent that they cannot be understood; if they be repealed or revised before they are promulgated, or undergo such incessant changes, that no man who knows what the law is today can guess what it will be tomorrow.

Many people have limited education in civics and the Founding documents.

There are, however, organizations that deal strictly in Constitutional education. You will benefit by going to their web sites. Constituting America has fun activities and contests for children as young as Kindergarten and on up to college age. Visit the National Center for Constitutional Studies for teaching tools and the Blackstone Institute that defends the Judeo-Christian world view of the Constitution. Educate others about these organizations that offer valuable information for all.

If you enjoy facts, *Newsweek* Magazine recently conducted a survey with 1000 citizens to find out how much basic knowledge of citizenship they had by taking the official US Citizenship exam. The result was staggering: 44 percent could not define the Bill of Rights, 73 percent did not know why the Cold war was fought, 29 percent could not name the Vice-President, and six percent couldn't circle Independence Day on a calendar.

This chapter does not teach specific facts of the Constitution, but facts that are necessary when defending the Constitution. The Declaration of Independence was intended by our Founding Fathers' to be the enforcer when using the Constitution. *The Federalist Papers* were written and used for further guidance in the original intent of the document. It is the Declaration which supports the right to life, liberty, and the pursuit of happiness based on unalienable rights that come from God. The Supreme Court in 1897 stated:

> The latter (Constitution) is but the body and the letter of which the former (Declaration of Independence) is the thought and the spirit, and it is always safe to read the letter of the Constitution in the spirit of the Declaration of Independence.

Many changes in our moral standards and legal system go against the "Laws of Nature and Nature's God" as stated in the Declaration. These words however were of utter importance to Sir William Blackstone who was an English judge and law professor who wrote the four volume *Commentaries on the Laws of England*. Many Founders such as John Adams, Thomas Jefferson, and James Madison held him in high esteem. It is important that people understand his influence on the writing of our Founding documents:

> When in the course of human events it becomes necessary for one people to dissolve the political bands which have

connected them with another and to assume among the power of the earth the separate and equal station to which the Laws of Nature and of Nature's God entitles them.

The Constitution is based on God's laws and natural law. Blackstone describes below the importance of the above statement that's crucial to the Development of American thought:

> Man, considered as a creature, must necessarily be subject to the laws of his Creator, for he is entirely a dependent being. And consequently, as man depends absolutely upon his Maker for everything, it is necessary that he should in all points conform to his Maker's will. This will of his Maker is called the law of nature. This law of nature, being coeval [coexistent] with mankind and dictated by God himself, is of course superior in obligation to any other. It is binding over all the globe, in all countries, and at all times; no human laws are of any validity, if contrary to this; and such of them as are valid derive all their force, and all their authority, immediately, from this original. The doctrines thus delivered we call the revealed or divine law and they are to be found only in the Holy Scriptures. These precepts, when revealed, are found upon comparison to be really a part of the original law of nature. Upon these two foundations, the law of nature and the law of revelation depend on all human laws; that is to say, no human laws should be suffered to contradict these.

Modern day scholars try to change the original intent of the Constitution based on these laws by claiming it to be an evolving document. The original intent was for the Constitution to be a stable force, not evolving. It's a solid set of principles of truth for every time and people. Justice Scalia was quoted in the *National Catholic Register* on February 17, 2007:

> The Constitution is not an empty bottle to be filled up by each generation. Over the past 40 or 50 years, the philosophy of a living, or evolving, Constitution has become popular.

> It is enormously seductive. You think everything you care about passionately is there in the Constitution. Everything comes out the way you want it to. Rights that never used to exist do, because the courts say so.

The Preamble of the Constitution sets its tone. It mentions six main purposes: promote a more perfect union, establish justice, insure domestic tranquility, provide for common defense, promote the general welfare, and secure the blessings of liberty to ourselves and our prosperity. In 1787 our Founding Fathers used "We the People" as a new beginning to offer people hope in a new nation. We can now do the same.

The Constitution is the law of the land. There is nothing that is superior to it. It allows our legal system to function and there is no other authority that can be used in its interpretation such as International law. Because its base is the Judeo-Christian worldview there can be no other worldview used to interpret it or be infused into it. It is obvious that judges cannot change its meaning and yet this is being done routinely.

There are certain principles that are an intricate part of the Constitution. They are: sovereignty, representative government, the rule of law, due process of law, equal protection of the law, private property, and free enterprise. The way that these are protected is through Federalism and the separation of powers. *The 5000 Year Leap* is a well-researched book and the author W. Cleon Skousen found 28 principles predominate in the Constitution.

The principles that were brought forth by our Founding Fathers are brilliant. There are few individuals that could ever match their intelligence and wisdom and because of it we see the magnitude of America's accomplishments. However, when we look at the massive amount of law that exists, it is evident that many are not in line with the Founding Documents and that is why our country is so off base.

Human arrogance has taken over and logic, reason, and God's authority is visibly absent. Let us remember the following when referring to the original intent:

> **John Adams**: The general principles on which the fathers achieved independence were the general principles of Christianity. Now I will avow that I then believed and now

believe that those general principles of Christianity are as eternal and immutable as the existence and attributes of God.

**James Madison**: We have staked the whole future of American civilization, not upon the power of government, far from it. We have staked the future of all our political institutions upon the ability of mankind for self-government; upon the capacity to each and all of us to govern ourselves, to control ourselves, to sustain ourselves according to The Ten Commandments of God.

The Declaration of Independence, as mentioned earlier, is crucial in reading and understanding the Constitution. Though the Constitution does not have God written in it, the Founders made it clear that the intent was for God and Nature to be the utmost authority in the rule of law. There are four fundamental rules of civil law. It is important that people accept this document and these laws:

- *The rights of man are God given and unalienable.*
- *The purpose of government is to secure those rights.*
- *The power of civil government is given by the consent of the governed who are entitled to rule also.*
- *A tyrannical leader forfeits his rule in order to restore the rule of law.*

The Constitution is of and by the people and thus it is the people's document. It governs the government after it's established. The Declaration and Constitution are based on God's law, natural law, the Bible, and the Ten Commandments. It gives everyone freedom, including all religions and atheists. Certain laws are in place to protect people from those who would abuse God given and natural laws. Let us examine the references to absolute truth in the Bible that help preserve the rights of everyone:

> Exodus 20:12-17…The Ten Commandments…"You shall not murder, steal, bear false witness, worship idols, commit adultery, nor covet thy neighbor's wife or goods."

Deuteronomy 30:19…"This day I call heaven and earth as witnesses against you that I have set before you life and death, blessings and curses. Now choose life, so that you and your children may live […]"

Psalm 119:4…"You have laid down precepts that are to be fully obeyed."

Hebrews 13:9…"Do not be carried away by all kinds of strange teachings."

John 14:6 "…I am the way and the truth and the life."

2 John 1:4…"It has given me great joy to find some of your children walking in the truth, just as our Father commanded us."

2 Timothy 3:16…"All Scripture is inspired by God, and profitable for teaching, for reproof, for correction, for training in righteousness."

2 Corinthians 3:17…"Now the Lord is the spirit, and where the spirit of the Lord is, there is liberty."

2 Chronicles 19:7…"Now then let the fear of the Lord be upon you, be very careful for what you do, the Lord our God will have no part in unrighteousness…"

The Founding Fathers knew the sinful nature of man. Thus, they incorporated the idea of three equal branches of government: executive, legislative, and judicial to keep our government from falling into tyranny. No branch would hold greater power than another. These are mentioned in the Bible, Isaiah 33:22. Thomas Jefferson clearly stated, "Let no more be said about the confidence of men, but bind them down from mischief with the chains of the Constitution."

# STEP 6
# COMMON SENSE

Recently I watched a mother on You Tube addressing her lawsuit against McDonalds for putting toys in Happy Meals. One must see humor in such actions for otherwise we would lose our minds with such nonsense. The absurdity of this situation is that there are many others of the same mentality working vigorously in using compromise for their agenda of change.

Transformation of America is happening not because of toys in Happy Meals, but because enforced diversity insists that all things hold equal value. This is a compromise of America's identity and destroys individual freedom. All that made this nation great is slipping away. The mother tells a tale of woe about her daughter's insistence on getting a toy each time a new one came out in the Happy Meals. Others were at fault for it.

The interviewer asked her about her role as a mother in letting her daughter have her way instead of saying "No" to her. The mother immediately gave herself victim status. McDonalds was the culprit. Their advertisements caused the arguments in the family over mom's "No" to the meals. She compromised her position of authority and blamed McDonalds for her own ineptness.

This is an example of entitlement thinking that demands change. Every person's crisis is used to deprive others of their liberty. The people promoting this type of lawsuit are the same ones who support education that indoctrinates people into victimization thinking, pushing them to make demands on society for phony rights. This is the real culprit that contributes to adult and children's mental, physical and spiritual demise.

We must pioneer in the re-education of God's Law, natural law, the

Constitution, and common sense. Unfortunately, common sense has been redefined and the principles are reversed to meet humanist agendas. Proper moral codes are now improper. Few use simple logic any longer. The Golden Rule has lost to expensive diversity programs which have shown no signs of greatly improving our nation, but diminishing it by encouraging anti-American policies.

We can't say that common sense is officially listed as such in the Constitution, God's authority, or The Ten Commandments, but it makes sense that if you follow the authentic rule of law you will be using common sense. Frederick Bastiat in *The Law* explains that the law cannot defend life, liberty, and property if it supports socialist policies. To carry out socialist policies, "legalized plunder" is necessary and thus, "the law is then perverted against the thing it is supposed to defend."

The above statement is an example of enforced diversity programs which protect special groups at the cost of others freedom. The Big Three have every right to be included in diversity status in order for it to be true to its purpose. The longer these groups are deprived of their rights, the longer our society allows plundering of individual rights critical to the rule of law. People buy into White Privilege and Wheel of Oppression education and in the name of justice make up laws that rob others of theirs.

Once again radical activists and lawmakers justify misuse of authentic law. We now have so many laws that go against common sense that the result is common folks are at the mercy of laws that few can begin to understand. Bastiat states the outcome of this below:

> Unfortunately, the law is by no means confined to its proper role. It is not only in indifferent and debatable matters that it has exceeded its legitimate function. It has done worse; it has acted in a way contrary to its own end; it has destroyed its own object: it has been employed in abolishing the justice which it was supposed to maintain, in effacing that limit between rights which it was its mission to respect; it has put the collective force at the service of those who desire to exploit, without risk and without scruple, the person, liberty, or property of others; it has converted plunder into a right,

in order to protect it, and legitimate defense into a crime, in order to punish it.

People are pushed into thinking they have no recourse. Diversity enforcement has done its job with many supporting the new laws, but in essence they are not in line with authentic rule of law and logical people know this to be true. Common sense motivates us to take steps to STOP the compromise. There are four common sense principles that are basic to our nation. We must promote them if we want to recover from the present chaos our nation is facing. They are below and can be attained by following the rule of law:

1. **Limited Government** – Thomas Paine stated that, "The government that governs the best is the government that rules the least."
2. **Fiscal Responsibility** – Increasing taxes, wasteful spending, and stimulus packages do not work.
3. **Free Markets** – In order for America to come out of our debt we must allow opportunity and small businesses freedom to create jobs.
4. **Constitutional Principles** – Our nation must adhere to the Constitutional principles to preserve life, liberty, and the pursuit of happiness and the solid base on which our nation was founded for survival of America.

The Tea Party promotes these principles upon which our nation was founded. The group is non-partisan and does not involve itself in social issues, but insists we must hold our representatives accountable for adhering to the above principles. However, the mere fact that they adhere to the Constitution does bring social issues to the forefront. The Tea Party members are excluded from diversity status because they dare to insist the above principles are better than others.

The Tea Party is bold in its position on the four principles, but many times their message gets lost because they are made the bad guy by redefined diversity education. The Tea Party movement saved the elections in 2010 and will be forever in the history books as an amazing feat. We must continue this work by using the STOP Movement and common sense. Steps seven through nine will provide quick responses to STOP the compromise of authentic rule of law.

# STEP 7
# RELIGIOUS AND SOCIAL RESPONSES

Quick responses will soon become part of your life. No more foolish statements from misguided people without you having a sound reply of truth. The reader must remember that the responses presented below are facts and common sense. You have no need to debate them. Stay in your absolutes, for this is the authority of God and natural law. Learn to use the truth with offensive attitudes, not defensive ones.

Present your statement in a pleasant manner. Never apologize for the truth. If you doubt any of it then you are compromised in some area of your life. Examine this closely, figure it out, and move forward. Chapters seven through nine are separated into religious, social, political, and economic questions and statements that many of us encounter daily. Quick responses will follow the questions. Practice them frequently and mold the responses to fit your personality.

The purpose of these replies is to give final authority to authentic rule of law. In this climate of anti-God, you will become more comfortable with your responses the more you use them. The ability to walk away from compromise solidifies your belief. It gives the listener time to think. Once the message is delivered there will be joy, for you have done the job successfully. The first section below provides statements that can be used in conjunction with some of your answers:

## GIVING AUTHORITY TO GOD:

1. Whether you are a believer or not, the truth is that America's laws are based on God's authority, natural law, and the Constitution.
2. God cannot lie because He is perfect. A wise man would follow His laws.
3. I didn't make the laws; an all powerful God did.
4. I choose to follow His laws for I do not want to stand before Him one day and tell Him I knew more than He did.

## GOD AND RELIGION:

- *How do we know there is a God?*
  **Response:** No one has proof there isn't a God. Look around you, for there are only two choices, either the universe and life came about by chance, or by intelligent design and we must choose one, but choose wisely.

- *God has nothing to do with our laws.*
  **Response:** If left to our own accord, any action man does to himself or others would be his decision which could lead to total anarchy. The Declaration of Independence is clear on the "Laws of Nature and Nature's God" as having everything to do with our laws.

- *God's laws are so restrictive that no one can enjoy life.*
  **Response:** God's laws give us unalienable rights, which grant us life, liberty, and the pursuit of happiness. It's common sense that if people follow His simple commandments, there would be no need for excess laws, restrictions would be less, and joy would be abundant.

- *We don't need religion in our society.*
  **Response:** You mean like secular countries Communist China or the Soviet Union that murdered over 130 million people? It's wiser to choose religion that keeps society in line.

- *We can act right without God.*
  **Response:** Every person has moments when reasoning gets cloudy. God's absolutes offer individuals a clear path to safety and security. When in doubt all we have to do is look to an all powerful God for answers and it surely takes the load off our shoulders.

- *Why can't we get order back in our nation?*
  **Response:** Arrogance now rules our nation and unless we become humble to a greater authority, America will continue to be in chaos and will self destruct. Hopefully America will not repeat the same mistakes as Greece and Rome, which caused their annihilation.

## BEHAVIOR:

- *I am so tired of people disturbing me in the movies with cell phones and talking.*
  **Response:** Stop being a victim. It's a symptom of society's breakdown and a loss of respect for others. You have the freedom to move to another seat, ask them nicely to be quiet, report them, or stop going to the movies; the choice is yours.

- *I can't stand it when God's name is used in vain.*
  **Response:** I agree so if the person is an atheist remind him with a simple, "I thought you did not believe in God," and for a Christian you can say, "Please do not say the Lord's name in vain in my presence or in my home."

- *It is unloving to judge others.*
  **Response:** You are right for we are not to judge the person, but we must judge the actions of others. Discernment is only logical for it is necessary for survival. It's actually loving to discern, for it keeps us safe from lifestyles and choices that are dangerous.

- *They had no choice. Look at the way they were raised.*
  **Response:** Many people have experienced hard times in

their lives, yet many come out of them. We must hold people accountable for their behavior. People do have choices. God gave us reasoning power through natural law and free will to make appropriate decisions.

- *Crude jokes upset me.*
  **Response:** Just put your hand up and say "STOP" and walk away.

## DRESS:

- *What's wrong with showing some cleavage?*
  **Response:** By flaunting cleavage a woman is pushing sexual arousal on men and giving mixed messages to them of her intentions. There are also men, women, and children that are embarrassed by it and find it distasteful, for it is difficult not to notice such an appearance. It's disrespectful of God's purpose of our bodies.

- *It's awful when women dress immodestly for church.*
  **Response:** It's distracting and upsetting. It has no place in church and is offensive to others. Ask your pastor, minister, or priest to provide clearer messages on modesty and the sanctity of the body, which is also beneficial to the offensive dresser.

- *I like my wife to show off her body.*
  **Response:** For what purpose? Do you want men to have immoral thoughts about your wife? What would God think of you encouraging others to covet your wife?

- *So what is so wrong with multiple body piercings, tattoos and stretched earlobes?*
  **Response:** People do not have to look at themselves, but others do. This type of body adornment is associated with primitive societies and an absence of, or loose morals. Many people find this offensive in a civilized society where we are to respect our God given bodies.

- *I am having a hard time because my children want body piercings.*
  **Response:** Make it easy and just say "NO." You are the parent and do not compromise your children, for God has given the responsibility of them to you.

## MEN AND WOMEN:

- *Patriarchal families do not give equal value to women.*
  **Response:** Of course they do for men value women and they usually make their decisions together. God however has clearly placed men as the patriarchal head of the family.

- *What has happened to our men of today?*
  **Response:** The National Association of Women (NOW) successfully pushes the feminization of men through diversity and sensitivity programs. When women decide they want their men back again and men decide to STOP cowering to this nonsense, our country will begin to mend and natural order will return.

- *We can't afford for me to be a stay at home mom.*
  **Response:** Can you afford not to stay home? Many families find that the cost for transportation, food, clothing, taxes, and childcare are expensive. With self sacrifice and change of lifestyle, lots of women find they can stay at home and fulfill what is just common sense and natural, which is for a mom to raise her children.

- *Women will find fulfillment once they gain independence.*
  **Response:** If independence means having two jobs, 24-hour days, home controversies, heavy stress, possible divorce, and guilt then where is the fulfillment? *The Paradox of Declining Female Happiness* reports that the more freedom, education, and power women have, the less happy they are.

- *Men and women are the same.*
  **Response:** God did make us different and with different purposes, but women have given up their uniqueness by trying to be like men. Many continue to label men oppressors.

Yet women oppress men when they support affirmative-action and female quotas in employment, whereby standards of physical tests are lowered, such as in the police force, fire departments, and military. Society must return to truth and stop the lie.

- *The Women's Movement gave women certainty of their rights.*
  **Response:** The rights were always there through God's authority, natural law, and the Constitution. The Movement supports anti-traditional policies that are destroying America. Women need to look at the power they have and STOP being replicas of Eve in the Garden of Eden.

- *Men are abusive.*
  **Response:** Not all men are abusive, but because of "oppression" mania, many men are falsely accused and found guilty. In reality both men and women can be abusive. Women now use an Order of Protection against the men and get sole child custody, plus more money. This does not require any proof of husband threats, or abuse. A woman can easily abuse the system and the man.

- *Many people cannot get out of abusive relationships.*
  **Response:** Yes they can; they just have to STOP. It takes hard work and discipline to leave such a situation, but God requires us to respect ourselves and our children. Staying in the situation only makes the abused an abuser also. There are many organizations available to help.

- *Feminists protect other women's rights.*
  **Response:** Where were the feminists when Terri Schiavo was thirsted and starved to death, or when Muslim women are stoned to death, and where are they for raped children, for Planned Parenthood does not report many of these cases to the police, yet some feminists support the organization.

## HOMOSEXUALITY:

- *Homosexuality is inborn.*
  **Response:** There is no study out there that has discovered a gene tied to homosexual behavior. It's a blatant lie and people have bought into it. God requires us to expose darkness and untruths.

- *Homosexuality is not wrong.*
  **Response:** That which is natural and right requires no explanation, but that which is disordered and unnatural requires an explanation and homosexuality is one of those. The Bible is clear in Romans that it is, "…unnatural, shameful, and a perversion," and in Leviticus it is called, "an abomination."

- *I get so mad at what homosexuals are doing to society.*
  **Response:** You have a right to be angry. They insisted all they wanted was to "have freedom to be who they are." Not so for they have used ruthless tactics to intimidate businesses, government, schools, boy scouts, Salvation Army, the military, and even churches to compromise their beliefs and policies for an acceptance of homosexuality as a normal lifestyle. Pray for them we must, but acceptance as normal, "No."

- *Homosexuals cannot change.*
  **Response:** Many have made the change and Dr. Spitzer at Columbia University did a 16 month study in 2003 of 200 individuals that improved from therapy and with no harmful effects. There are many other studies, but they are hidden from public knowledge.

- *There must be a gene for homosexuality even if we cannot find it.*
  **Response:** What you are saying is that there is a gene for abusers, child molesters, murderers, thieves, phobias, overeaters, masochists, sadists, alcohol and drug addictions, and every other imaginable thing; for it's just not true.

- *If a gene does not cause homosexuality what does?*
  **Response:** Dr. Jeffrey Satinover M.D., has studies that indicate some of the following: children are born with traits that are more masculine or feminine than actual gender; the child is different, which causes distancing from dad and pushes yearnings for same sex attention; a doting mother; and of course child molestation.

- *People are hateful and angry toward homosexuals.*
  **Response:** The act is an abomination because it goes against what nature intended for our body parts. People are falsely labeled hateful when they respond with normal reactions that are not hateful, but truthful statements about this lifestyle that are not in line with natural law.

- *What is wrong with homosexuals adopting children?*
  **Response:** It's abusive to push a role model of this behavior onto a child, for it's against God's laws. Dr. Hansen, a clinical psychologist, has studies that indicate children raised by homosexuals have a seven percent higher chance of living the homosexual lifestyle.

- *There are so many people who are homosexual.*

- **Response:** Only two to three percent of the population is homosexual. They falsify numbers as being more than they actually are in order to win people over to believing it is a normal lifestyle. Having to work so hard to convince 97 percent of a population that natural law includes homosexuality is proof unto itself that it is immoral and against the laws of nature.

- *Homosexuals are only defending themselves.*
  **Response:** The fact that homosexuals have to argue that it is true is proof that it is not true for as Shakespeare said, "Me thinks that you protest too much," thus the guilty one protests all the time because the argument is invalid or incorrect.

- *What possible harm can homosexuals do to society?*
  **Response:** David Tyree, New York Giants receiver in 2011,

couldn't have said it better "...if you trace back even to other cultures, other countries, that will be the moment where our society and itself, loses its grip with what's right. Marriage is one of those things that is the backbone of society." When the family unit goes; so goes society as we know it.

- *Shouldn't homosexuals be allowed to serve openly in the military?*
  **Response:** They serve in the military, but what they now seek is recognition for their lifestyle. We allowed open homosexuality into our traditional military units. Now our courageous men and women must compromise and attend sensitivity classes to learn proper standards of behavior toward homosexuals. After all they maybe sleeping next to them and even showering with them. Our military must focus on their jobs, not homosexuality.

- *I could care less if homosexuals get married.*
  **Response:** You should care because God's law is that marriage is between one man and one woman. Common sense and natural law could not be clearer on the truth.

- *If two homosexuals love each other why can't they get married?*
  **Response:** Love has nothing to do with it, for you can love a dog, but you cannot marry him. Marriage is for one man and one woman. This is God's law, natural law, and just common sense.

- *Homosexuals say that they are monogamous just like heterosexuals.*
  **Response:** Studies show otherwise. They have an average of 50 sexual partners whereas heterosexuals have four. Less than two percent are monogamous as compared to 83 percent for heterosexuals and common sense tells us that they will say this to encourage people to support homosexual marriage.

- *Homosexuals are discriminated against.*
  **Response:** In June of every year, the California State Capitol Rotunda is decorated with rainbow colors and life size figures of homosexuals; parades, museums, months, and safety laws are dedicated to them; over 50 percent are college graduates, while the general public has 16 percent; they hold a large

number of managerial positions; they contribute large sums of money to Obama fundraisers; and they can even marry, but it has to be someone of the same sex. They are not discriminated against.

## LIFE:

- *It is not really alive until it is three months old.*
  **Response:** Science is clear on the fact that it takes 23 chromosomes from a man and 23 chromosomes from a woman to come together and form a zygote. This completes the DNA to make up a human being. A child has this at the moment of conception. Plus, a baby's heartbeat begins to beat 18 days from conception and brainwaves can be detected as early as 6 weeks from conception. It's common sense that it is human and alive.

- *There is nothing in the Constitution that says we must protect life.*
  **Response:** There is due process of law and equal protection of all people under the Fifth and Fourteenth Amendments. If a person is tried for double murder when a woman is pregnant then this must be a human being with equal rights.

- *It is more humane to take an abnormal child's life than to let it live.*
  **Response:** Do we change the definition of murder because of an affliction? God expects us to uphold the dignity of life, no matter the circumstances. Some want to even "murder" children up to one year. Where do we draw a line? It is not up to us to choose who lives or dies, for we are not God.

- *Women have a right to choose.*
  **Response:** A woman makes her choice when she has sexual intercourse.

- *I don't believe in abortion except if it is a result of incest or rape.*
  **Response:** In other words an innocent victim pays the price for the crime of another for this is contrary to our system of justice that states a person is not convicted until he or she

has, "…a right to a speedy and public trial by an impartial jury."

- *It is more humane to abort in a legal setting than in the back alleys of America.*
  **Response:** Murdering a child is inhumane no matter where or what the circumstances are. It is murder.

- *A baby does not feel an abortion.*
  **Response:** By 9 weeks from conception, all the structures necessary for pain sensation are functioning. Besides, you might say that to do such a deed is like the Aztecs who ripped hearts from people's bodies to give honor to the Gods, for we allow a baby to be ripped apart to honor a woman who has given herself the godly power of life and death. This is evil.

- *I wish our country could go back to the way it was.*
  **Response:** So do many good people who face such things. With the time you have left you can aid in recovering some of the old America. We must return to God and authentic rule of law. A good start is to protect our born and unborn future citizens.

- *The media stated that Terri Schiavo wanted to die if ever faced with a debilitating injury.*
  **Response:** There is no proof and nothing written that states this. The only person who claims she said this was her husband. Many people say this, but change their mind when actually in the situation.

- *What Terri Schiavo's husband did to her was inhumane.*
  **Response:** Society led the way with abortion and euthanasia and Teri is the result. She showed all signs of responding to therapy following her horrible incident. Her husband however had different ideas and withdrew therapy. Then he barbarically thirsted and starved her to death. All the while America watched it on their television screens.

- *Planned Parenthood cares about women and helps them.*
  **Response:** Margaret Sanger, the founder, really cared, but she cared about getting rid of black people and those she

thought not deemed worthy by using abortion, and now the black race has submitted willfully to slavery for they have the highest incidence of abortion.

- *We must treat animals with respect and dignity.*
  **Response:** We must be kind to animals, but animals do not have human rights and must never be placed above human beings. To do so is against God's purpose of man having dominion over the animals.

## DIVERSITY:

- *We have the right to do what we want.*
  **Response:** Liberty is not doing everything one wants to do, but not doing everything one wants to do so everyone can have authentic freedom. Nowhere in the Constitution does it give anyone the right to do anything they want.

- *There is nothing wrong with diversity.*
  **Response:** I totally agree as long as it is natural diversity, but there is nothing right about redefined diversity that insists all ideas, values, morals, ethics, lifestyles, religions, and personally held beliefs hold equal value, except mine.

- *Diversity is about loving others.*
  **Response:** How about Judeo-Christians, European descendents, and traditional patriots get some love? Redefined diversity judges them and falsely accuses them of being hateful because of their beliefs. The Ten Commandments tell us not to "… bear false witness against thy neighbor."

- *Why has diversity become so popular?*
  **Response:** It's an addiction. Read *Diversity Addiction: The Cause and The Cure* and you will see why brainwashing works. People compromise their beliefs for what they think is a greater good. They become addicted to the group love given them by their compromise and the addiction begins. They must continue to compromise in order to receive the

love that feeds their addiction. Diversity addiction is just as bad as other addictions.

- *Conservatives tend to blow things out of proportion.*
  **Response:** There is a real threat to our freedoms when Judeo-Christians, European descendants, and traditional patriots are discriminated against because their beliefs are what formed the basic foundation of America.

- *No reason to get all upset about diversity.*
  **Response:** Thomas Paine once stated, "A long habit of not thinking a thing wrong gives it a superficial appearance of being right."

- *Certainly the diversity programs are not doing anything wrong?*
  **Response:** Are they doing anything right? In California over 100 districts are showing no improvements in education and no studies indicate that enforced diversity programs are improving test scores.

- *Do people have to take diversity programs?*
  **Response:** We are not living in Nazi Germany or Communist China, but in the United States of America, so just say "No." You have God's authority, natural law, and the Constitution to support you and that is all you need.

# EDUCATION:

- *There is nothing wrong with sex-Ed classes.*
  **Response:** It's actually abusive. Sex has become a priority and many teens ignore their school work. A high rate of disease and out of wedlock pregnancy continues. HIV infects two teens every hour of every day, 18,000 yearly; the Human Papilloma Virus (HPV) infects 1,000,000 yearly with 25 percent teens; homosexuals carry over 50 percent of the AIDS virus and make up only two percent of the population; and we have 1,000,000 yearly teen (ages 13-19) pregnancies. Common sense tells us that "taboo" and abstinence education would be safer.

- *Is redefined diversity education really that bad?*
  **Response:** It's anti-American, anti-God's authority, anti-natural law, anti-Constitution, anti-common sense, anti-tradition, and anti-moral. It's not only bad, it's treasonous.

- *Can't people do anything to stop discrimination against traditional Americans?*
  **Response:** You surely can't if you don't start, so get moving and stand in the truth of authentic rule of law, which is God's authority, natural law, and the Constitution. You have a right to speak out. We must educate people to know that for diversity to be true to its purpose it must accept traditional people, complete with their beliefs.

- *Isn't tolerance a good thing?*
  **Response:** America thrives on tolerance. Education centers across America demand it. We now tolerate murder through abortion, thievery, adultery, lust, perversion, abusiveness, lies, cheating, and other things we used to hold wrong? We even tolerate Communism and Socialism claiming them equal to Capitalism. We tolerate just about everything in our country except education in the truth of what is the best, which is the American way.

- *Is homosexuality being taught in classroom material?*
  **Response:** It has been for a long time and not just in the classroom, but in government, businesses, churches, and even homes across America. Marxists use the homosexual agenda to cause chaos, such as SB 48 in California, which requires homosexual, transgender and bisexual role models be included in the Social Studies books for children, Kindergarten and up. This is blatant child abuse.

- *What is the Day of Silence?*
  **Response:** The Day of Silence is in thousands of schools across America once a year in the springtime. It allows homosexuals to be silent all day in classrooms and wear signs and pass out literature that they have been silenced for too long by society. This is against school codes and civil

rights of others. The Free Exercise Clause of the Constitution protects children from coercion in the classroom. The Supreme Court case *Lee v. Weisman* says that, "Even subtle pressure diminishes the right of each individual to choose voluntarily what to believe."

- *Homosexuals claim their lifestyle is not harmful to children and must be included in classroom education.*
  **Response:** Check out the Center for Disease Control. They've reported that homosexuals lose up to 20 years of life expectancy, while cigarette smokers lose 13.5. Homosexuals carry a high disease rate for HIV, syphilis, anal cancer, and Hepatitis B and C. Schools must STOP indoctrinating little ones to believe this lifestyle is safe.

- *I am too busy to get involved right now.*
  **Response:** A great proportion of citizens are brainwashed into believing America is the bad guy. Do you have time not to do anything to save America from them? How will you answer your children and grandchildren one day when their freedoms are gone? Most importantly how will you answer God?

# STEP 8
# POLITICAL RESPONSES

**EQUALITY:**

- *People are equal.*
  **Response:** The Declaration of Independence, common sense, and God tells us that people are created equal and they remain so as part of the human species, but they do not remain equal as individuals, for each person is unique and uses their talents in different ways; some excel and some do not. This is simple logic.

- *Aren't people entitled to equal things?*
  **Response:** It will be almost 200 years since Thomas Jefferson said in 1816 that we must, "…guarantee to everyone the free exercise of his industry and the fruits acquired by it," but it is the *Communist Manifesto* number one that requires abolition of property, and number three that abolishes inheritance in order for everyone to have equal things. Many still do not want communist thinking ruling America. No, people are not entitled to equal things.

## MORALITY AND RELIGION:

- *Morals do not belong in government.*
  **Response:** The Founding Fathers were clear on morals being included in government in order for it to survive. Without morals included in the decision making process our human nature takes over and this can lead down many dangerous paths.

- *Jesus had nothing to do with our law.*
  **Response:** Our Founding Fathers were all God fearing leaders and believed in the precepts of Jesus Christ as being the best for this country's laws, but history revisionists will not tell the truth of the Founders stand on Christianity. In fact our country is intimidated into not even mentioning His name in public. Could it be that Jesus is a threat for He never compromised right and wrong?

- *Thomas Jefferson did not believe in Christianity.*
  **Response:** Thomas Jefferson authored a work for the Indians entitled *The Life and Morals of Jesus of Nazareth*. It is the teachings of Jesus set forth in the Gospels. Common sense tells us this is a person who believes in Christianity.

- *Religion cannot be a part of politics because there is separation of church and state.*
  **Response:** Unfortunately people now believe this. The truth is that a letter was written by Thomas Jefferson in 1802 to the Danbury Baptist Association of Connecticut. The term "separation" meant that government could not infringe upon them a state established church. Our Founding Fathers were clear that God was an important part of government.

- *Why are church leaders not speaking out at the pulpit?*
  **Response:** Church leaders have been silenced. There are many reasons for their compromise: some buy the lie of redefined diversity, some believe separation of church and state applies to the pulpit, and some fear losing their tax status. They no longer speak of sin. Whatever the reasons,

churches must return to God's law in order to bring our country together under one God.

- *The divorce rate is skyrocketing in America.*
  **Response:** Society has allowed our moral codes to be "educated out" of daily life. Recent studies show that 40 percent of people do not believe in marriage. Noted married public figures participate in perverted sexual and adulterous behavior. This is a tragedy for the American family has always been a stabilizing force for our nation. The Commandment "Thou shalt not commit adultery" is clear on not coveting another's mate and for good reason, to preserve the family unit.

## TACTICS:

- *It is respectful to use gay instead of homosexual.*
  **Response:** Not so. They purposely changed the name to "gay" to take the attention off of the behavior for a political ploy. That's hypocritical and we must return to using homosexual just as we use heterosexual.

- *Look at what happened to Harvey Milk due to his homosexuality.*
  **Response:** There is no proof he was murdered due to his homosexuality, yet this myth allowed laws passed for statues, a museum, and a school day to role model this man. This was brilliant on their part, for they used an untruth to advance the homosexual movement.

- *We must provide material in various languages for different ethnic groups.*
  **Response:** Why, because political correctness says so? In reality doing this is enabling, for now they say 2 out of 5 families do not speak English and this is a grave injustice. This puts our country at risk. It's also not cost effective and is disrespectful to America.

- *The Muslim Religion is a peaceful one.*
  **Response:** There are about 1.2 billion Muslims in the world.

Some estimates claim that 10-13 percent are radicalized, which means that about 120 to 180 million Muslims throughout the world are terrorists or sympathizers.

- *Don't you agree that profiling is wrong?*
  **Response:** It is a perfectly logical thing to do. When segments of a race, culture, or religion are the majority in propagating a particular evil then it is proper reasoning to profile. The safety of our nation depends on it and the fact is the majority of terrorists are Islamic.

- *Most people realize that America needs change.*
  **Response:** Many people want change. They bought into Obama's promises as positive change, but instead he redefined change to be socialist policies. Now many people want a real change that will return us to the Constitution and traditional moral values.

- *It's a conspiracy theory that deception occurs in diversity programs.*
  **Response:** Seeking Educational Equity and Diversity (SEED) is a worldwide diversity program that uses over 20 methodologies behind closed doors. They are typical of most diversity programs that want to transform the beliefs of attendees. The facts are presented in a book called *Seeds of Deception: Planting Destruction of America's Children*. These programs are wrong and deceptive.

- *Haven't good things come from compromise?*
  **Response:** Compromise gave us the "Great Society" with many on welfare and fatherless families; it gave us Medicare and The New Deal which is bankrupting us, and it opened the door for North Korea to get nuclear weapons and now Iran. Not good, but America did not compromise their separation from King George. This gave the Founding Fathers a strong base to compromise amongst themselves making possible the Constitution.

## RULE OF LAW:

- *The Constitution is supposed to give us rights.*
  **Response:** Our rights have always been there and they are natural rights, but the Constitution does not give us our rights; it protects the right to provide oneself and family with life's necessities.

- *It takes forever to try and change laws.*
  **Response:** You are right, so we must be vigilant to bills that are like Obama's Patient Protection and Affordable Care Act and not add one more to the list, and then we must make use of our freedom to vote out those who initiated them.

- *If we have laws allowing abortion then it must be okay.*
  **Response:** These laws are not authentic laws, but immoral ones, which are against all we know to be right according to natural law and God's authority. We do not have to obey this law or contribute to those who perform them.

- *Why can't Muslims use Sharia law?*
  **Response:** They can in countries that allow it, but it is not American law and in order for a law to be authentic it must adhere to God's authority, natural law and the Constitution, and Sharia law is barbaric and cannot be a part of our rule of law.

- *Legislation must be passed to protect homosexuals against bullying.*
  **Response:** Many people make this statement and need to use logic in this area. There are many laws already in place for this protection, so there is no need to duplicate laws, only adding to the overabundance we already have in place. The truth is that with every new law homosexuals are pushing for an acceptance of their way of life.

- *Thank goodness we still have our First Amendment rights.*
  **Response:** A gentleman in Holland is on trial for hate crimes because he dared to say something negative about the Koran and some in America are promoting hate crime legislation for this type of speech. This is dangerous and we must be

bold in standing for our First Amendment rights. Contact your representatives and do not be silenced.

- *Why do we have so many laws?*
  **Response:** Some people believe they are entitled to what others own without having to work for these things. Others believe their own moral code needs to be legislated. They have no regard for authentic rules of law or the future of our society.

- *There is little we can do about the abuse of the law.*
  **Response:** There is much you can do. Become part of the STOP Movement; vote out those who promote bad laws and vote in God fearing leaders. You can join grassroots' organizations, educate others, write letters to editors, fax and lobby your representatives, screen your child's education, take them out of public schools and instead home school, follow God's way, and enjoy being a political activist.

# OPPRESSION:

- *People cannot get away with hateful speech.*
  **Response:** So what is hateful speech, for according to the Supreme Court decision in *Cantwell v. Connecticut* the words must be said, "directly to the person, face to face, with a powerful enough impact to disrupt the peace of the environment in order to be fighting words." In reality the truth is deemed hateful by those who do not want to hear it.

- *I have to be silent about my opinions on homosexuals.*
  **Response:** No, for we have the First Amendment and equal protection of the law to speak our beliefs, plus the word of God that we are not to stand in darkness, but present truth.

- *Why should Homosexuals be deprived of marriage?*
  **Response:** Use common sense, for why should a man who wants to marry four women be deprived of it, or why should

a man not be able to marry an eight year old, and why should a man who wants to marry his dog not be able to. They are not deprived of equal rights to get married as long as it is with one person, of age, human and the opposite sex.

- *What happened to California Proposition 8?*
  **Response:** The people voted twice against homosexual marriage and yet still the will of the people is being undermined by activist judges. This is oppression of the people for the rule of law has been replaced with judicial supremacy. This is wrong and the people must stand up to it.

- *They accused me of being hateful.*
  **Response:** STOP being a victim and accepting accusatory words for slander is a serious thing, dangerous to one's job, and future, and is seditious and evil doing and you can insist that they STOP it by using lawful measures that are guaranteed you by the rule of law.

- *There is no hope of ever getting our country back again.*
  **Response:** You don't have to be a victim, for we are guaranteed equal rights under the Constitution, but the rights don't come easily, so muster up some energy and let's take back America or else we will lose it forever for our children and grandchildren.

- *I just gave up on voting.*
  **Response:** Just look at what the Tea Party did in 2010 because of voters. Not voting is an act of oppressing yourself, for you are making yourself a victim to others who vote in someone you may not like or want in a position of authority.

- *The military are visibly absent as role models.*
  **Response:** You are right. It is time to start showing them due respect. Every person can make a difference by defending and supporting our troops. There are many wonderful on-line sites for contributing to the cause and you can make recommendations in your city council and schools to bring the role model of our military back to life again.

- *America pushes our politics on other countries.*
  **Response:** America shines its light as the best freedom ever for other countries to emulate. We do not push our policies, but instead extend our help to Countries in crises. America will do what is necessary to protect freedom, even if the policies are frowned upon by some. We must never apologize for being Americans.

- *Airport searches are for our safety.*
  **Response:** You think you're safer because they may scan or strip search your body and others, but terrorists can still go undetected by machines and scans if they have inserted a destructive device into a body cavity. The so called preventative measures waste a lot of tax payer money and only give the illusion of security.

- *It is not against our rights to be searched at airports.*
  **Response:** People at airports are treated like criminals until proven they are innocent by unreasonable search and seizure procedures which are against our Fourth and Sixth Amendment and let's not forget it's against our moral code to have someone touching our bodies and those we love.

- *The white people are responsible for slavery.*
  **Response:** The truth is that slavery goes back thousands of years when Black Africans and Arabs enslaved ancestors of today's African-Americans. Slavery continues today perpetrated by cruel acts and power hungry blacks that oppress their own people. White people actually freed the slaves. A good movie to watch on this is *Amazing Grace*.

- *Thank goodness the Constitution has Civil Rights laws.*
  **Response:** Yes and we need to use them for all people and stop paying $60,000 and up yearly to bring in skilled teachers to instruct in White Privilege education that discriminates against the white race.

- *Oppression is everywhere in America.*
  **Response:** People are taught they are victims by charts of oppression. White, male, heterosexual, rich, able bodied,

and Judeo-Christians are deemed oppressors; people of color, female, homosexual, poor, disabled, and non-Christian are classified as oppressed. This chart separates rather than joins people. According to Justice John Roberts, Jr. in the Supreme Court Case *Parents Involved in Community Schools v. Seattle School District* "…the Government must treat citizens as individuals, not as simply components of racial, religious, sexual orientation, or national class."

- *What is the Wheel of Oppression?*
  **Response:** It is a teaching tool. Put the letter "P" in the center of a wagon wheel, which represents "privilege." Then use education that classifies people as oppressors or oppressed. Place the oppressed groups on the wheel spokes and tell them that they have the right to be in the center of it with the "P." This produces entitlement attitudes that insist on new laws that give them what they want without the right to have it. God commands us to not "…covet thy neighbor's goods."

- *White Privilege education is the truth.*
  **Response:** White Privilege education is a lie and fabricated by Marxists seeking the transformation of America. It is discrimination against the white race and unlawful, for it is against civil rights laws and education codes. Read *White Privilege and The Wheel of Oppression: The Hoax of The Century* to understand how widespread this education is across America and the devastation it is causing our country.

- *What are Sustainable Development and Agenda 21?*
  **Response:** They share the same agenda, for they take away our freedoms and property under the misconception that their planned developments will make the world a better place for the future. They are grounded in the United Nations and use the Wildlands Project and Smart Growth for the collective good by taking away individual rights.

## RACE:

- *There is nothing to show that white people are to be included in Civil Rights laws.*
  **Response:** Are the white people not a race? So why would we not be included? The Supreme Court in *Bowen v. Missouri* stated that the pendulum swings both ways and recognized that white people are discriminated against by race.

- *The white race is given certain privileges.*
  **Response:** This is an opinion and not fact, for all races are given equal rights, but the truth is that privileges are taken from whites due to affirmative action.

- *Social Justice is good for society.*
  **Response:** Depends on what you mean by social justice and society. It is not social justice when Attorney General Eric Holder did not prosecute the Black Panthers when they intimidated white voters in Philadelphia, and when the Dayton police department exams were lowered for people of color who could not pass it. This is bad for America.

- *All people of color and ethnic groups ever wanted were to be included into society without it being the focus.*
  **Response:** That was the original intent, but now they classify themselves according to their color or ethnic group in clubs, political groups, Miss America contests, education, specified months, television stations, and even accomplishments? This is not common sense.

- *Martin Luther King Jr. was a truly great man.*
  **Response:** Yes he was authentic and a great man, but now some black leaders and people have made a mockery of him for they use skin color to gain power, jobs, education, and money without the individual achievement of it. This was not Martin Luther King's dream.

## GUNS:

- *Guns are dangerous.*
  **Response:** The gun is a tool to be respected, but some people who use them are careless and dangerous. Children dying from gun accidents, under age 15, are 200-300 a year. However, swimming pools show up to 950 a year, car accidents are thousands every year, and bicycles are over 600 yearly. We do not however stop people from owning swimming pools, cars, or bicycles.

- *I am fearful of guns.*
  **Response:** There is nothing to fear, for if used properly they can be used for recreation purposes, hunting, collecting, competition, stress reduction, and the security of our Second Amendment rights.

- *Gun rights come from the Second Amendment.*
  **Response:** The right of self defense is a basic natural right. The Second Amendment was put in place to protect that right and the Supreme Court in 2008 (*Heller Case*) supports our Second Amendment rights.

- *The "people" in the Second Amendment does not mean the individual, but the collective militia.*
  **Response:** The Second Amendment is debated often and recently went to the Supreme Court for clarification. The Heller Case in 2008 supports an individual right to bear arms. One must look at the language of the times and see that the Founding Fathers used "people" to mean an individualist interpretation just as in the First Amendment. There is nothing to indicate anything to be different in the Second Amendment.

- *The Supreme Court made guns legal and now no one will take them away.*
  **Response:** Be careful when you say this because though the Supreme Court ruling in 2008 assured us of our rights, the

next court could just as easily take them away. We must be ever vigilant.

- *Surely there has to be some gun control?*
  **Response:** How far does it go? America has compromised its natural right for self-protection and opened its doors to more restrictions. How do we stop it when they come to confiscate our guns? Who says when it stops? This is dangerous territory.

- *Why does anyone need a gun?*
  **Response:** They're fun number one, but most importantly to keep a tyrannical government in check securing our freedoms and to prevent a foreign take over.

- *It's dangerous for people to be carrying guns.*
  **Response:** Not so, for statistics prove that the states that allow carrying guns, such as Florida, have lower crime rates. This makes sense, for people deal with each other by reason and by force. When people are put on the same playing field, such as a woman with a gun against a strong man using force, then common sense tells us that a gun makes it safer for her and for society. There was a rush to purchase guns spurred by the fear of Obama's election in 2008 and the violent crime rate actually decreased by six percent between 2008 and 2009.

- *Are a few things stolen worth killing the robber?*
  **Response:** Most people are not mind readers. They do not know if the intruder will or will not kill them. It is proven that one out of three intruders will harm the residents, plus protecting your family is in line with God's laws and the Second Amendment rights of every law abiding citizen.

- *How could anyone shoot another person?*
  **Response:** It is never the same until it happens to you, for if you saw someone entering your neighbors' house and they were going to shoot someone, you may not shoot them. If they entered your home and were going to shoot your children, you may change your mind and pull the trigger.

- *What's the big deal if we have to give up our guns for the safety of others?*

  **Response:** This is very dangerous thinking. It does nothing to keep anyone safe for it already dictates that guns are dangerous, rather than the people using them. The bad guys will not give up their guns, but if our guns are taken from us so goes all of our freedoms and any hope of safety.

# STEP 9
# ECONOMIC RESPONSES

**ENTITLEMENT:**

- *It's loving to take care of others.*
  **Response:** We must be careful of how we mean loving, for it can promote dependency which is in conflict with the principle of "subsidiarity" by which we respect the inherent dignity and freedom of the individual by never doing for them what they can do for themselves.

- *We have to have welfare.*
  **Response:** Ronald Reagan said, "If we subsidize something we will get more of it; if we tax it, we will get less." There are more efficient and beneficial ways to help people than by handouts. If welfare works, then let's get everyone in the world on it, but how would that work?

- *Guess we have to pay for their abortions.*
  **Response:** Thomas Jefferson said, "… that to compel a man to subsidize with his taxes the propagation of ideas which he disbelieves and abhors is sinful and tyrannical," and I think this says it all.

- *The government has to take care of the poor for they have rights too.*
  **Response:** The poor have the same rights as everyone, but the Constitution doesn't require the government to take care of the poor. Christians are required by God to take care of the poor. Individuals, churches and organizations such as Salvation Army do this job. There is no government "right" to take from the people and redistribute the wealth.

- *How did people ever come to believe government should take care of them?*
  **Response:** They're taught it every day and everywhere by entitlement education that robs them of their creative spirit and dignity, which then leaves them little chance to ever take care of themselves. This is a grave offense.

- *Our black grandparents did not get reparations, so it's okay for us to get entitlement money.*
  **Response:** Where did you learn this entitlement thinking? Every wrong does not require compensation. Countries would fold up if they had to compensate everyone for back grievances. It also enables future generations, which is a serious wrong.

- *It's great that government takes care of the Indians.*
  **Response:** Not so, for some Indian reservations are operated with entitlement thinking. Programs continue popping up that have done nothing to advance individual responsibility, but only dependency on hand outs. This devalues human beings.

- *It's sad that many black women with children have men who do not live up to their responsibility and many times leave their family.*
  **Response:** What is sad is that we have to pay for their choices, whatever their race. In 2010 the illegitimacy rate was 41 percent. Federal and state welfare handouts were 900 billion. Many of these women look to Big Brother and vote in those who will subsidize them. If the checks quit coming, common sense tells one that the problem will be solved.

## FISCAL RESPONSIBILITY:

- *How can someone tell you what to do with your property?*
  **Response:** Marx and Engels in *The Communist Manifesto* state, "The theory of communism may be summed up in the single sentence: Abolition of private property." Eminent domain, the green movement, high property taxes and capital gains taxes threaten property rights. Our government has put into force czars that dictate environmental standards that are out of line with common sense. We must vote out our representatives that plunder laws depriving us of authentic property rights.

- *We just have to increase taxes.*
  **Response:** Why and how much is enough? The rich are condemned and punished for being successful. In 2005 the top one percent paid approximately 39 percent of all U.S. taxes, the top ten percent paid about 70 percent, and the top 25 paid 85 percent. Overall, the top 50 percent of taxpayers paid 96 percent of all U.S. taxes. In 2009, 47 percent paid no federal income taxes and the bottom 40 percent received the cash benefits. The Constitution supports limited government that leaves us our money to spend. It's common sense that raising taxes is destructive to the economy.

- *I trust our government to get us back in shape again.*
  **Response:** The only way this will happen is for people to pay attention to fiscal responsibility, free market, limited government, and constitutional principles. The people must have a STOP attitude and hold our officials responsible for getting this nation back in shape again. If not, vote them out.

- *What is the problem in taking a bit more from those who have more money?*
  **Response:** There is not a problem, for government takes it easily, but the problem is that individuals get punished for hard work rather than getting rewarded. This is not right

and indeed is stealing, which goes against natural law and God's authority.

- *President Obama needed a stimulus package to save America.*
  **Response:** His stimulus package did nothing to save the country. Instead we raised the debt even more and the 14 trillion debt only gets worse as government gets more involved. We must return to free market and fiscal responsibility, for they work and that is just fact.

- *Sometimes the government has to step in to save the country like President Roosevelt in the Great Depression.*
  **Response:** They now believe that he actually extended it by seven years, for UCLA economists Harold L. Cole and Lee E. Ohanian show that anti-competition and pro-labor measures Roosevelt signed into law as part of his New Deal slowed what could have been a much better recovery.

- *Our Government must give money to poorer countries.*
  **Response:** America gives more money to poor countries than any other. We are in severe debt so it makes no sense to borrow more money from China to give even more money to other countries so that it will add to our debt and that of our children and grandchildren.

- *Well at least we are safe because we have three separate government branches.*
  **Response:** Yes this works if it's a moral government, but right now our government extends its power by adding departments which blends the legislative with the judiciary to make many new laws that allow the Federal government to regulate education, housing, energy, and agriculture which increases the national debt, plus it's against the Constitution.

## ENERGY:

- *All the new energy programs will surely save us money.*
  **Response:** Most energy programs do not save us money

such as the smart meters that charge for the meter, cost the workers their jobs, and then tells us we can save money as long as we do not use it during peak hours. Many of these programs are costly to implement. The initial investment will take many years to prove to be cost effective.

- *We must find ulterior ways for energy production.*
  **Response:** You mean more debt for something that is working just fine like the enormous cost for growing corn for ethanol when it is cheaper to use our own oil or nuclear energy; or building mass transit railways when cars are cheaper and work just fine; or closing down West Virginia coal plants because of outlandish new EPA standards and whereby losing over 600 jobs and increasing electricity cost by 10-15 percent. This is not fiscal responsibility.

- *Why shouldn't corporations go to China where production is so much cheaper?*
  **Response:** One simple reason, we're supporting the growth of Communist China and destroying ours. We need to make it lucrative for companies to stay in America and vote in representatives that will get manufacturing back in America. After all, God did give us proper reasoning, so let's use it.

- *We don't have enough oil so we must use foreign sources.*
  **Response:** This is not true, for we have an abundance of oil in America, but President Obama will not grant permits for drilling in our country, but instead gives billions of dollars to Columbia to support their own oil refineries.

- *The "Green" movement is good.*
  **Response:** The green movement promotes earth rights over human rights all the while ruining our economy by extreme EPA standards that increase costs to develop green energy, which puts many companies out of business. It's good to serve political favors, for people who support it are given the business contracts for energy over those who support traditional energy forms.

- *Carbon Dioxide is bad.*
  **Response:** Tell that to a tree or plant, for the truth is that the more carbon dioxide we have the greener the world is and by reducing the carbon dioxide we are stunting the growth of trees and plants.

## ILLEGAL IMMIGRATION:

- *Even illegal aliens have the right to food, shelter, education and health care.*
  **Response:** America must use wisdom in immigration. We cannot take in everyone. In the state of California, illegal alien benefits have bankrupt the state and caused irreparable damage to businesses and hospitals across the state. These made-up rights are used to get votes from those who vote according to race and according to entitlements thinking.

- *There are enough jobs for everyone.*
  **Response:** If there were enough jobs for everyone then the unemployment rate would not be rising to unprecedented highs. It's common sense that when you have 20 to 30 million illegal aliens in this nation, they are going to take jobs from citizens.

- *We should have open borders.*
  **Response:** Open borders leave our country vulnerable to crime, chaos, drugs, and bankruptcy. You lock your doors for safety and so should America to protect our citizens and rule of law. Tell your statement to the many who have loved ones and friends murdered by illegal aliens.

## COMMON SENSE

- *There are too many powerful people in government to ever make changes.*
  **Response:** Not really, for there are 100 senators, 435 congressmen, one President, and nine Supreme Court justices. That's only 545 human beings responsible directly,

legally, morally and as individuals for the nation's economic problems. There are over 300,000,000 people and if they use proper reasoning then they will know who to vote out of office.

- *It is humane to take care of illegal immigrants children.*
  **Response:** Our country has murdered 53,000,000 future paying citizens, which is one-fourth of the work force for those under the age of 40. This is not humane, nor is it common sense to support illegal immigrants' unborn children who will take from our system, rather than pay taxes.

- *I wonder how we could improve our economy.*
  **Response:** Four simple solutions that the Tea Party promotes are a sure thing: free market, fiscal responsibility, limited government, and constitutional principles. It's just common sense that this will get us out of debt.

- *Homeschooling produces anti-social children.*
  **Response:** There are no studies that show any negatives of homeschooling. On the contrary all the studies show them socially intact and consistently scoring higher on test results than public school attendees. Common sense tells me from these results that the children are well-adjusted.

- *It's important that women get the same salary as a man.*
  **Response:** That is logical for if they are doing the same work then the same pay is only fair. What's interesting is that when women entered the workforce in the last century men's salaries decreased. Two people now must work in a family to bring in the salary that one man brought home in the past. This is not common sense economics.

- *Women are oppressed in the work force.*
  **Response:** Look around you. Women are no longer oppressed. Women have some of the highest paid jobs in the country and they surely have a presence, if not the power, in all job forces throughout our nation including high government positions.

- *Global warming is real.*

  **Response:** Global warming is nonsense. It is untruthful rhetoric. Global warming has been around since the beginning of time and is cyclical. Now power hungry people use fear tactics to control the masses. They are succeeding as we hear people who want to return to primitive ways of living to save the planet. Do some smart investigation and common sense will take over.

- *I can't stand to shop in stores where the clerks have multiple piercings and tattoos.*

  **Response:** Did you write the store to let them know you will stop shopping in it if they do not listen to your pleas to be more respectful of the shopper? Society will adapt to those who stand for their beliefs and let them be heard.

- *How can we get Christmas back in the stores?*

  **Response:** Let the store know you will not shop there anymore if they do not use Merry Christmas. Get others to do it too. Customers make a difference. God makes it clear in the First Commandment that we are to have no other gods before Him. Jesus' birth is the priority at Christmas.

- *How did this all happen to America?*

  **Response:** We abandoned God's authority, natural law, the Constitution, and common sense. Read *Seeds of Deception: Planting Destruction of America's Children* and it will give you the necessary facts to understand how the last 100 years affected the authentic rule of law.

# STEP 10
# STOP THE COMPROMISE

People who work against authentic rule of law will never compromise. When I lobbied an ex-Senator at the Capitol who happens to be lesbian, her aide was good at debate. We had intense one on one about abortion and homosexual effects on society. In the end the aide was clear it didn't matter what anybody said or wanted, the Senator would vote the way she wanted. He laughed when I told him that she works for us.

What was interesting is that he could not get the upper hand with me as he tried every trick to get me to compromise my beliefs. It did not work because by then I had mastered the ability to think clearly when involved in emotional subject matter and used STOP tactics. The only way to get people like her out of office is to vote them out. In the meantime we can push our arm forward mentally and say STOP to the compromise at opportune moments.

No more lies, insults, deceit, and theft of our rights. We don't have to accept victim status. Contrary to redefined diversity, we have the best rule of law and with it we will take back America. The Ten-Step Guide helps you enjoy the process. Get hooked up again to the days of yesteryear. Rent some old cowboy movies. The traditional values in *The Rifleman* are perfect for the young. Our grandchildren love cowboy movies. Angela and Michael know the good guys from the bad guys and point their conduct out to us.

My husband and I find great joy in watching *Wagon Train* and hearing God's name mentioned in reverence, as well as the Lord's name in prayer as they pushed across the plains in the wagon trains. We must return to the pioneering days. It was hard work, but the benefits were many. Who will reeducate others in the truth, if not you? Why not lighten the workload and STOP the compromise. It's not only joyful to do, but fun to watch our opponents' reaction.

Visualize the Lone Ranger and listen for his distinct, "Hi-Yo Silver, Away!" as he rides the range with his Indian companion Tonto, defending goodness. Get out your cowboy hat and boots and ride a new frontier. With open fields to cross and barriers to cut down, the American spirit will rise again. It shouts STOP to those who dare to question God's authority, but for all who believe in the authentic rule of law, truth will lead the way. The galloping of horse's hoofs will only get louder. The STOP Movement has just begun.

# ABOUT THE AUTHOR

Georgiana Preskar is the Founder and Executive Director of Diversity Reform USA, the Director of Eagle Forum of Sacramento, and has served on the Sacramento Republican Central Committee. She authored *Seeds of Deception: Planting Destruction of America's Children*, *Diversity Addiction: The Cause and The Cure*, and *White Privilege and The Wheel of Oppression: The Hoax of The Century*.

Her traditional Chicago suburban upbringing with dad, mom, and brother, gave her knowledge of America's heritage and appreciation for its Judeo-Christian foundation. As a mother, homemaker, registered nurse, sociologist, substitute schoolteacher, real estate agent, religion education instructor, and prayer coordinator, she observed through the years a noticeable change in the American way due to enforced diversity programs.

Through radio talk shows, speaking engagements, educational seminars, in-home discussions, workshops and her writings, she educates those in doubt as to their right to be accepted into diversity status complete with their beliefs. She promotes the belief that men are born equal, but ideas, values, morals, ethics, lifestyles, religions, or closely held personal beliefs are not equal.

With two grown children and four grandchildren under age five, Georgiana encourages protection of children for survival of America. In 2010 Georgiana became an NRA Certified Instructor in Basic Pistol and Refuse to Be a Victim classes in support of the Second Amendment. With her husband Michael of 36 years, she continues to battle for the last frontier of freedom, the USA.

# REFERENCES

1. Armstrong, Virginia; Ph.D. "Revive the Constitution." <www.BlackstoneInstitute.org>.

2. Barton, David. *Original Intent.* Texas: WallBuilder Press, 2000.

3. Bass, Joseph L. *A Little Handbook on the Second Amendment: What the American Aristocracy Does Not Want You To Know.* The Down Home Enterprise, December, 1999.

4. Bastiat, Frederick. *The Law.* Alabama: Ludwig von Mises Institute, 2007.

5. *Cantwell v. Connecticut.* 310 U.S. 296, 60 S. Ct. 900, 84 L. Ed. 1213, 1940 U.S. 591.

6. *Catechism of the Catholic Church.* New York: Costello Publishing Company, Inc., 1992.

7. Drummey, James J. *What Do You Say I* AM? Massachusetts: C.R. Publications Inc., 2008.

8. Farrar, Doug. "Super Bowl hero's shocking same-sex marriage comments." http://sports.yahoo.com/nfl/blog/shutdown_corner/post/Two-former-Giants-see-same-sex-marriage-very-dif?urn=nfl-wp2653

9. *Lee v. Weisman.* (90-1014), 505 U.S. 577 (1992).

10. Kitsch, Abraham I. "The Moral Code for Youth." *The National Weekly*, Collier's: 1925.

11. *Life Application Study Bible; New International Version.* Illinois: Tyndale House Publishers, Inc., 1919.

12. Marx, Karl, and Engels, Frederick. *The Communist Manifesto.* New York: International Publishers, 1969.

13. McIntosh, Peggy. "White Privilege: Unpacking the Invisible Knapsack." <http://www.promoteprevent.org/resources/white-privilege-unpacking-invisible-knapsack>.

14. *Parducci, v. Rutland.* 316 F. Supp. 352, 355 (M.D. Ala. 1970).

15. *Parents Involved in Community Schools v. Seattle School District No.1.551 U.S. 701* (2007). Wikipedia. <http://en.wikipedia.org/wiki/Parents_Involved_in_CommunitySchools_v._Seattle_School_District_No._1>.

16. Preskar, Georgiana. *Diversity Addiction: The Cause and The Cure.* Indiana: AuthorHouse Publishing, 2007.

17. Preskar, Georgiana. *Seeds of Deception: Planting Destruction of America's Children.* Indiana: AuthorHouse Publishing, 2005.

18. Preskar, Georgiana. *White Privilege and The Wheel of Oppression: The Hoax of the Century.* Indiana: AuthorHouse Publishing, 2010.

19. Reese, Charlie. "545 vs. 300,000,000 People." *Orlando Sentinel*, March 9, 2009.

20. Robert, Michael T. *Sex in America.* Massachusetts: Little Brown Publishing Company, 1994.

21. Romano, Andrew. "How Dumb Are We?" *Newsweek,* March 20, 2011.

22. Satinover, Jeffrey M.D. *Homosexuality and the Politics of Truth.* Texas: Brown Books Publishing, 1996.

23. Schlafly, Phyllis. "The Cost to Taxpayers of Missing Fathers." http://www.eagleforum.org:80/column/2011/june11/11-06-17.html

24. Skousen, W. Cleon. *The 5000 Year Leap.* National Center for Constitutional Studies, 2006.

25. Schindler, Robert and Mary. *A Life That Matters.* New York: Warner Books, 2006.

26. Stevenson, Betsy, and Wolfers, Justin. "The Paradox of Declining Female Happiness." *American Economic Journal : Economic Policy 2009* http://bpp.wharton.upenn.edu/betseys/papers/Paradox%20of%20declining%20female%20happiness.pdf

27. *The Supreme Court and First Amendment Rights of Students in the Public School Classroom: A Proposed Model of Analysis*, 12 Hastings Const. L. Q. 1, 2o (1984).
28. *The U.S. Constitution And Fascinating Facts About It*. Illinois: Oakhill Publishing Company, 2004.
29. "Understanding Whiteness, Recognizing Privilege Conference." University of Massachusetts. April 17, 2004. <http://whiteprivilege.hampshire.edu/bios.html>.
30. Unruh, Bob. " 'Gay' family kids 7 times more likely to be homosexual." *World Net Daily*, June 08, 2009.
31. Wexler, Bruce. *The Wild West Catalog*. Philadelphia: Running Press Book Publishers, 2008.

www.ingramcontent.com/pod-product-compliance
Lightning Source LLC
Chambersburg PA
CBHW022129170526
45157CB00004B/1802